COLONELS OF WISDOM

A DAUGHTER'S REFLECTION ON LEADERSHIP

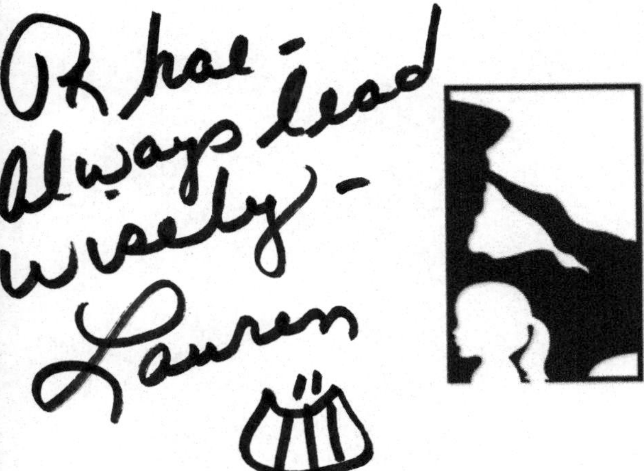
Always lead
wisely –
Lauren

Lauren Ann Schieffer, CSP

LSE Publications
Bonner Springs, KS

Lauren Ann Schieffer, CSP/LSE Publications
Bonner Springs, KS
www.laurenschieffer.com
Book Layout ©2018 BookDesignTemplates.com
Ordering Information: info@laurenschieffer.com
Quantity sales. Special discounts are available on quantity purchases by corporations, associations, and others. For details, contact the "Special Sales Department" at the email address above.
Colonels of Wisdom - Leadership/ Lauren Ann Schieffer, CSP. —1st ed.
ISBN 978-0692112694
Photo of father and daughter by Tech. Sgt. Nadine Barclay, courtesy of U.S. Air Force
Photo of saluting airman by Senior Airman Kedesha Pennant, courtesy of U.S. Air Force

What others are saying about Colonels of Wisdom

"With the first quote of this book I came to respect The Colonel, and to admire his daughter for sharing this wisdom. Make this book your companion and apply these ideas to transform your life to one of greater achievement and higher meaning."

Jim Cathcart, CSP, CPAE
President, The Cathcart Institute

"*Colonels of Wisdom* is a wonderful read filled with powerful lessons for business and life. Endearing and heart felt, its insights can apply to both executives and young adults."

Lt Col (ret) Waldo Waldman, CSP, CPAE
Author of the national bestseller, *Never Fly Solo*

"I have read tons of books on the topic of leadership and found *Colonels of Wisdom* to be both inspiring and refreshing. Within the endearing messages shared between a father and his daughter, are insightful leadership lessons that encourage and challenge the reader to become a better leader."

Lethia Owens, CSP
CEO of Game Changers International, LLC

"Lauren Schieffer has written a very touching book, but it's far more than just an emotional journey. This book challenges many of the notions in our current culture. It shows clear and concise path to true success in leadership."

Steve Diggs,
Founder, Fast Forward Leadership

"Psychologists and researchers have shared that, 'Leaders are a product of the influence of their fathers' presence in their lives.' Lauren Schieffer has demonstrated, through this book, how the impact of her father has shaped her as a leader. Now, as a role model, she shares those leadership lessons to help future leaders."

Ed Robinson, CSP
President, Robinson Performance Group
Author of *4 Giant Steps toward Leadership*

"My over-riding thought as I read *Colonels of Wisdom* was my wish to have been able to have talked with Lt Col Leigh. Thankfully, his leadership, wit and wisdom live on and are strengthened by the stories and examples Lauren shares. I am sure you, like me, will be posting the Colonels quotes on your walls as reminders of our responsibilities as leaders."

Jim Pancero, CSP, CPAE
The Powerhouse of Sales

Dedicated to the memory of The Colonel
Lt Col Gerald G. Leigh, USAF Ret
Scholar, Visionary, Father, Mentor, Leader

Introduction

My father, Lieutenant Colonel Gerald G. Leigh, was a bit of an anomaly in the United States Air Force. He put 36 years into the Air Force without flying any combat missions. He was a private pilot, but his eyesight was too weak for deployment. Instead, Dad put his other strengths to use in serving our country. He had advanced degrees in civil, mechanical and chemical engineering. During his mid-career years (once I was old enough to ask "what Daddy does"), he led a team of engineers at the Weapon's Laboratory on Kirtland AFB in Albuquerque, New Mexico. There he worked on facility survivability and measuring building damage through bombing runs in the New Mexico desert. His focus was defining optimum altitude for each ordinance, in order to provide maximum damage on selected targets with minimal periphery damage.

Later in his career, he was the Division Chief for the Flight Dynamics Laboratory at Wright Patterson AFB in Dayton, Ohio. There he was instrumental in designing and refining the advanced-composite materials for the B-1 (stealth) and the F-series fighter jets. When he retired from the Air Force, Dad took a position as Senior Research Engineer for the New Mexico Engineering Research Institute at the University of New Mexico and was a founding member of the New Mexico Solar and Wind Energy Association.

Calling Dad "The Colonel" started sometime after he was promoted to Lieutenant Colonel. It began with my mom just being sassy with him. After Dad retired, it became a term of endearment.

The Colonel, died on the 30th of December 2006. As is the case with most, if not all, fathers, he had been a primary influence on my life and the person I grew to be. To say I was a bit adrift after his death is an understatement. I would hear his voice in the back of my head so often during those first few months, and sadly, I could not help but focus on the reality that I would not hear that voice again. That was the impetus for me to begin writing down the things my father told me. It helped to ground me during that first year and became part of my grieving process.

My first book, *Road Signs on the High Road of Life*, grew out of the eulogy I gave at his memorial and stands on its own as a collection of life lessons. But as time went on, I realized there were so many other things I needed to remember, and so I began to collect them in a single document. I called them "Colonelisms." As my collection grew, I realized they were naturally grouped into a few categories: leadership – what it means to be a leader; accountability – self-discipline and responsibility; and significance – how to live a life of impact and dream big.

I had originally thought to simply turn this collection over to my children so they could better remember their "Grandpa Ho Ho," so I was a bit taken aback when a colleague asked if he could have a copy of my collection.

Within a month, three other people made the same request. That's when I decided I needed to publish Dad's wisdom.

I have offered insights in this book on what each of these quotes mean to me and how they can be applied in life and business. That doesn't mean these are the only correct interpretations of my father's wisdom; they are simply mine. I have decided to publish this in three volumes, as the three categories revealed themselves to me: Leadership, Accountability and Significance. These three concepts go a long way toward defining who The Colonel was and what he tried to teach me. I have narrowed each category down to fifty-two quotes so they can be utilized as a year-long study—one per week—if desired.

I have specifically written these quotes as I remember my father saying them. That means the grammar is not always perfect, and they are peppered with many "kid's," "kiddo's," "young lady's," and other addresses my dad used when he spoke to me. I hope you will indulge me in that and read the wisdom through it. There is a lot to be learned from The Colonel. I hope you get as much out of it as he would have hoped.

This is my absolute favorite picture of my dad. Taken up at our cabin in 1969. I am tucked safely under his arm and, as always, he is working (note the pen in his hand and the pad in his lap). This picture more than any other defines our relationship.

"Take it from me, kid. Being bigger doesn't make you better.

Being bigger means you HAVE to be better because more eyes are on you all the time."

The Colonel was 6'6.5" tall and 285 pounds on his leanest day. He had a personality that entered a room five minutes before he did. But, Dad never depended upon his size to intimidate others or get his way. He believed that because of his size, much more was expected of him. He believed he had to be kinder, make better choices, and lead by example all the time *because* he was so visible.

One of my favorite football players of all time, J. J. Watt, stands 6'5" and weighs in at roughly 290 pounds. There is no question that he is a large presence in any space he occupies. On the football field, it's his job to intimidate and bring players down with his sheer size. Off the field, however, Watt is an incredible leader—in his words and his actions, in the way he gives of his time, in his kindness and soft smile, and in the respectful way he treats everyone he comes in contact with. Watt knows that because of both his size and his celebrity as an elite athlete, people are watching him and looking to him to show the way, off the field as well as on the field. J. J. Watt lives up to that challenge every day.

By the same measure, I think it might be too easy for someone small of stature to assume they are not seen and that therefore they can get by with small lapses of judgment or improprieties. Never think that. Mahatma Gandhi measured only 5'5" and topped off at 140 pounds, but he never let his small size prevent him from leading a nation to independence.

He knew that a small voice, placed consistently in the right place with the correct message, could change the course of history.

It's our responsibility, regardless of stature, to conduct ourselves as if someone is watching us all the time.

"Leadership has nothing whatsoever to do with the title you hold. Leadership is an inside job. Leadership is a choice."

As I have traveled and spoken to thousands of companies across the globe, I have discovered that being a manager, supervisor, team leader, or even a president or CEO does not make you a leader. I have met many people with such titles that were in no way leaders—merely people higher on the organization chart that made more money than those below them on that chart.

The Colonel knew that leadership is not a position, but an action. He encouraged me to be a leader in every role I took on.

In school, he taught me to be a classroom leader through how I conducted myself, through my participation, and through my study habits. That doesn't mean I was ever the best student. (I certainly wasn't!) It means he expected me to try harder than others, to be mentally present, and to put in my best effort at all times. He also expected me, whenever and in whatever way possible, to facilitate others' learning.

When I began my first job right out of college as a receptionist, he started talking to me about "leading up" and letting my bosses know the best way to keep me motivated and engaged in the vision of the company. He encouraged me to share ideas I had respectfully and not to be discouraged if they weren't acted upon immediately.

He taught me to endeavor to make my boss look good and be a "subordinate partner" in the company's success.

When I did step into management, Dad encouraged me to create an environment wherein my staff could grow, to empower them to make their own decisions, and to support them professionally, emotionally and intellectually.

When I stepped away from "Corporate America" to work for myself, Dad consistently challenged me to lead those I spoke to so they could become leaders as well.

Leadership is a choice. It's a decision you make every day, exhibited in what you say and what you do, regardless of the position you hold.

"Leaders don't look for recognition from others; leaders look for others to recognize."

Near the end of my term as president of a non-profit foundation award committee, I made a joke to Dad about how the awards should all go to me because I had worked harder than anyone else on the committee or in the arts community that particular year. "*Wrong*," was The Colonel's response. "As president, it's your *job* to work harder than anyone else. Don't look for recognition for that. It's part and parcel of the title."

Few people step into leadership because they want to hide in the shadows. I don't think wanting to be acknowledged is about an over-inflated ego. I think it's a fairly normal and natural desire to be recognized for our hard work and our successes. Leaders, though, have to rise above that very natural desire. What we need to be constantly aware of is that recognition comes in many forms. It's not always immediate, and it might not be public. Recognition of successful leadership may very well come in intangibles—in the form of an amazing corporate culture and high productivity or spin-off leaders.

When things go well, it is crucial to give credit and accolades to everyone who had even the smallest part in that success. The crucial key to this, though, is that it must be authentic. There is a massive difference between acting humble and being humble. When you consistently and genuinely recognize others for the team's success, it creates a desire in them to repeat that success and generates long-term results. That long-term result will always, in one form or another, be accredited to the leader.

Dad continued, "Instead of looking for credit, you should be entirely focused on who you should be giving credit to. You didn't achieve this year's success on your own. Far from it, kid. It's not the leader's job to get the recognition, but to give the recognition. Besides, if you are always focused on helping your team look good, they will invariably make you look good."

"Leadership is not a place you get to, kiddo. Leadership is a journey you live."

The last time our children were locked in a car with us was a long-weekend trip from Kansas City to Chicago when both of them were in high school. Because my husband hates interstates and loves to "see what's out there," we meandered our way north on side roads. We stopped in Ottumwa, Iowa, to see where the M*A*S*H character Radar O'Reilly was from. We visited Riverside, Iowa, to see where Captain James Tiberius Kirk will be born on March 22, 2228. We went to Dyersville, Iowa, to lob a ball or two on the Field of Dreams, and we stopped in Rockford, Illinois, to see the Rockmen Guardians who guard the ford of the Rock River. We did all of this before we finally pulled into Chicago. What would have normally been an 8-hour drive took us almost 16 hours, and the kids were *so* ready to be done with the adventure! But, what a great experience it was. What do we now know about Iowa and all those other places that we will never forget?

Are we there yet? That annoying mantra uttered by every child on a long-distance trip sums up the way many people see leadership—as a destination.

Unfortunately, if you have that mindset, once you do obtain a leadership position, you will stop working for it and working at it. If, on the other hand, you look at leadership as a consistent journey, then you will always be taking the opportunity to be flexible, to learn, to see things from a different perspective than you expected, and to visualize "what's out there" for your team.

"An achiever wants to see themselves rise to the top. There's nothing wrong with that, but it's not leadership. A leader wants to see those around them rise."

Growing up in the shadow of The Colonel, with all his commendations and his advanced degrees, it was understood that I would or should be an achiever. I thought I needed to be more, do more, and be at the top of every pile I was thrust into. That is not necessarily a bad thing, but as I was struggling to lead a Mary Kay unit that was not achieving as much as I was (or as much as I thought they should), Dad pointed out that achievement is not necessarily leadership.

The way I saw it, if they were not achieving their full potential then I needed to achieve more. I needed to lead by example and show them how it's done. I thought that if they could see me achieving, they would know how to do it themselves and be eager to emulate it. Now, there is some sense in that. Mary Kay Ash always said, "The speed of the leader is the speed of the gang." But it certainly wasn't working that way. During one particularly difficult month, my senior director told me that my unit wasn't working because everyone in it was content to sit back and watch the "Lauren Schieffer Show." I was furious. I huffed and hollered and told her that she just didn't understand the dynamics of my particular unit. At the time, I was completely unwilling to recognize that my showboating style was not effectively leading my unit. It was not leadership; it was personal performance.

I needed to shift my focus away from my own achievements and onto helping them achieve. I needed to work with them, to support and teach them how, rather than assuming that by watching my accomplishments they would "see" how to achieve. Most of the time, leadership requires that we walk, not in front of, but beside our team, gently supporting and guiding as they grow.

"You don't have to know everything, kiddo. Don't pretend to. Surround yourself with people you trust to know what you don't, and be willing to do the work to learn."

The Colonel was one of the most intelligent people I've ever met. My sister is as well and has multiple advanced degrees in engineering. But, neither Dad nor my sister knows everything. No one knows everything. Your leadership will improve once you realize you don't have to know everything and you don't have to pretend that you do.

In the late decades of the 20th century, it was a common business practice to recognize where your weaknesses were and then work hard to shore up those weaker areas. If you could learn more and gain more skill in those weak areas, the conventional thought was that you would be more valuable as an employee and as a leader. It wasn't until Strength Finders and similar companies began to gain popularity that this belief changed and people started focusing on their individual strengths. That shift made me *so* happy!

I am a communicator, negotiator, creative visualizer and team cheerleader. Profit and loss, depreciation, amortization, payables, receivables, total cost assessments and all that other accounting "schtuff" make my brain hurt. I am so much more effective as a leader when I have someone I trust who knows and loves all the numbers stuff and will handle it for me. I allow her to do her thing and trust she will tell me what I need to know.

If you're honest about what you don't know, your team will respect your honesty. Then, it's important for you to trust those who *do* know and, if it is in the best interests of the team, be willing to learn those things. Sometimes, though, it is not in the team's best interest—the leader needs to trust the experts and move forward based on their expertise and advice.

"Leadership is not a license to do less. Leadership is a responsibility to do more."

It is a common but misguided perception that once you've "made it to the top," things get easier because you can relax and let other people do the work. That is an excellent recipe for losing your spot at the top. Being a leader is hard work—all the time. It is also rewarding—most of the time. And that "most of the time" makes the rest of the time worth it.

The Colonel loved this quote, which he said was originally from General Douglas MacArthur: "Never send your troops in where you are not willing to go, and never ask them to do something you are unwilling to do yourself." While doing everything yourself is not a characteristic of leadership, if you have never been where you're sending your team (metaphorically) then you have no basis to guide them on the journey.

I have a friend who is a fitness trainer. He spends eight to ten hours a day in the gym with his clients, guiding them to their fitness goals. Every evening after dinner, he goes back to the gym to work out himself. I asked him about that one time:

"You're in the gym *all* day long. Don't you get tired of being here?"

He said, "Of course I do. But my clients won't put work in that I haven't put in before them. Can you imagine if I was 50 pounds overweight, always out of breath and looking like the most I could curl is a donut up to my mouth? Would you believe me when I told you that you could achieve your personal best? Would you push just a little bit harder when I encourage you to? I put the work in on myself, so I can guide and encourage you to put the work in on yourself."

Then he told me to do another set of ten...

Leaders do more than the rest of the team—usually behind the scenes—and not for their own achievement or accolades but for the benefit of the team. Leadership is a lonely road that requires letting go of privilege in order to build something permanent—a legacy.

"You can't take credit when things go right if you're not willing to accept responsibility when things go wrong."

One of Dad's favorite quotes was supposedly from legendary college football coach Bear Bryant: "If the Tide wins big, the team did a great job. If we squeak by with a win, I've got some work to do. If we lose, it's all on me." The Colonel was very adamant about the leader taking responsibility rather than credit. It is the leader's job to give credit to the team when they have done well and when they have achieved or exceeded a goal.

During one of Dad's terms at the Weapon's Laboratory at Kirtland AFB in Albuquerque, he was in charge of a division called Facility Survivability. Dad's team was responsible for testing the effectiveness of an individual bomb, or series of bombs, dropped on a structure. One of the early tests they performed out in the New Mexico desert was considered an overwhelming success. The instruments they had set up to measure force and expansion, ground compression and debris patterns had worked perfectly. The Air Force, therefore, had the information they needed to calculate the most effective altitude for their bombing raids in Vietnam. Dad was given a commendation, but he refused to accept his until every member of his team was also given their commendation.

Leaders also don't place blame on others. Harry Truman's famous quote "The buck stops here" was another one of Dad's favorites. The year after Dad's successful ordinance test, a second test was assembled in the desert. This was a larger acreage test, requiring more time and more investment to set up. Dad and his team worked on construction and instrumentation for over four months. When the bombers dropped their payload, the explosion was impressive and could be heard over 100 miles away. Unfortunately, not one of the instruments set up to record the effects of the explosion did their job. A single wire connection had come loose sometime before the test, and it had disabled all of the instrumentation. While Dad had not put the connections together himself, he shouldered the entire blame. It had ultimately been his responsibility to make sure each connection was solid—was checked, double checked, and triple checked. He had failed his team and cost the USAF a great deal of time and money.

Two important, yet very different, sides of the same coin exemplify one of the most important characteristics of leadership: giving credit to the team when things go well and being willing to take responsibility, with grace, for the team's shortcomings.

"Don't consider yourself irreplaceable. *No one* is irreplaceable, kiddo.

In fact, if you are doing your job, you are constantly trying to create your replacement."

The primary objective of leadership is not team accomplishment. It's not building numbers, or dollars, or figures, or accolades. The true goal of leadership is building up new leaders. Your job as a leader is to replace yourself—and the more times you can do that, the better.

When Mary Kay Ash designed her cosmetics company, it very quickly became a model upon which most reputable modern-day direct sales companies were modeled. Mary Kay knew that if someone achieved the position of Sales Director by recruiting consultants into the company but did not encourage those recruits to become directors themselves, eventually that director would have a unit too large to lead. More importantly, when she retired, her unit would be without a leader. Mary Kay often quoted Zig Ziglar, "When you help enough people achieve what they want in life, you will achieve what you want in life." With that in mind, she established a career path that encouraged her leadership to spin off additional directors from their units, or they could not move themselves any further up the ladder. By consistently working to replace themselves, directors could build and grow multiple capillary leaders to share the load. They moved ahead and received greater rewards while their recruits also moved ahead and received greater rewards, and the company grew exponentially.

As leaders, it's our job to give each member of our team the opportunity and resources to grow into their own leadership style. Some will rise to the challenge and others will not, but all should be given the opportunity. Your reputation as a leader will grow in proportion to the number and quality of new leaders who rise with you.

"You are only a leader if others are willing to follow you, not because they have to, but because they choose to."

Although he only lived to see the first three, Dad loved the *Star Wars* movies. He loved the example of the two Jedi enemies, Darth Vader and Obi-Wan Kenobi. You would think that, because of his size, he would identify with the imposing and ominous force of Darth Vader, but not so. He wanted to be everyone's Obi-Wan.

Lord Vader ruled (led) by fear and intimidation. When someone questioned or disappointed him, he took immediate, often violent, action to correct or remove the dissenter. If someone was promoted to a new position because his predecessor had been removed, they rarely felt very confident in their position! While this is fiction and I can't imagine someone ruling an office with the same Vader-esque force (pun intended), I have encountered many managers who endeavor to keep their team safely and quietly under their thumb. This management style quickly squelches anyone's initiative to speak up, question procedures, or offer ideas.

Obi-Wan Kenobi, on the other hand, led with patience and by earning and giving respect. He encouraged but did not force (again, pun intended!). He believed in Luke Skywalker before Luke believed in himself. He consistently and gently encouraged Luke to push his limits and expand his expectations. And, when the time came, Obi-Wan "took one for the team" in the most profound way possible, knowing that his strength was needed more in the cosmic realm than in the physical.

Sometimes it may seem that leading with intimidation is an effective way to get results immediately. Managers who have reached a point of desperation will often resort to threats and intimidation to get what they believe is productivity. Unfortunately, if your team fears you, the last thing they are going to do is communicate openly with you. This can cause a breakdown in results and productivity, not to mention morale and longevity. Threats and intimidation may be a management style, but they are not a leadership style.

When you lead with patience and respect, you inspire your team to think for themselves, work together, communicate and achieve more. This creates a team where people come to work every day because they want to. They follow you because they trust you and choose to be led by you.

"You never succeed alone. There is always someone supporting you."

You've no doubt heard the saying, "Teamwork makes the dream work." Although a bit cliché, it is undoubtedly true. Precious little in this world is achieved through solo efforts. Athletes in individual sports such as golf, boxing, swimming, and track all have a team of trainers, coaches, doctors, and physical therapists helping them. That doesn't even take into account the team that designed and built the equipment they use.

When my daughter was in middle school, she joined the swim team. It gave her an opportunity to exercise and be competitive while doing something she loves—swimming. Although Melissa was never the fastest, she was a solid competitor and an integral part of the team. Unless you are on a relay team, swimming is an individual sport—one swimmer in their own lane pushing for everything they're worth. And yet, no one on her team achieved anything on their own. There was the head coach and the assistant coach. There were a couple of team captains and seasoned swimmers mentoring the newbies. And, each swimmer's individual placement and times combined to produce the overall team score during a swim meet.

When Melissa was named co-captain her senior year, there was a younger swimmer, Barbie, who was lightning fast. This sophomore was a water-moving machine who helped carry the team to state competition that year.

Toward the end of the season, in the weeks leading up to State, Barbie experienced a bit of a slump. I encouraged Mel to help lead her out of it. Melissa said, "I don't have anything to tell her, Mom. She's better in the water than I am. Her technique is impeccable, and I'm not even in her league."

You're right," I replied. "But you are the team captain. You need to support her in other ways. As a leader, what *can* you tell her?"

After thinking about it for a minute, Mel said, "She has the mechanics. She just needs to get back in the right head-space. I can remind her what a champion she is. I can paint the vision for her of what it's going to look like when she breaks the state record, and I can tell her how proud the whole team is going to be of her when she wins more individual events than anyone in team history. I can tell her how proud I will be tagging off to her as she anchors the four-by-four and the four-by-two. I think *that's* what she needs right now."

Barbie absolutely crushed it at State. She achieved all the records she had hoped to, and every single person on the team played a part in her success.

A great leader is important, and a great support staff can make or break an organization. If the team feels like they are all contributing and are being recognized for that contribution, everyone succeeds.

"You'll know your team is weak when they work against each other, for themselves or to curry your favor.

You'll know your team is strong when they work with each other, for each other."

When I was in high school, Dad and I lived by ourselves for a year—just the two of us. During that year, he taught me a great deal about teamwork and leadership.

Every day there would be a list of things that needed to be done: homework, vacuuming, dusting, emptying the dishwasher, laundry, etc.—the basics of running a household. I walked home from school every day and was expected to get started on that list. But, so many times, Dad would come home from work and find that nothing had been done. As a teenager, I didn't have much motivation to get work done in his timeframe. I had the natural surly sloth many teenagers have during those years. I know it must have frustrated him.

Dad often used our favorite sport, football, as a teaching tool for me. "We are a team," Dad explained, "like a football team. If the quarterback can't count on his offensive line to do their job when they need to do their job, then he's going to get sacked every time. The offensive line doesn't have the luxury of saying, 'I know. I need to block for you. It's on the list. I'll get to it... eventually.' The same goes for the defense. The defensive tackles can't say, 'Yeah, I see him. I'll get over there and bring him down at some point.... Get off my back about it.'"

"Every player on the team," he went on, "needs to do what he needs to do when he needs to do it, or the team falls apart. If we are going to be a team, Lauren Ann, I need you blocking for me. More importantly, I need you blocking for me when you are supposed to be blocking for me, not in your own time in your own way."

An office team, just like a football team, is not just a bunch of people working side by side in the same place, with each person focused on getting their own work done. A true team is accountable to themselves and each other, working with each other and for each other so that the whole achieves more than the sum of the individual parts.

"Don't be afraid to show your flaws every now and then. They're what make others want to work with you."

If you're anything like me, this one is tough. This was (and is!) such a hard lesson for me to wrap my brain around. When we look in the mirror (whether real or proverbial) and see our faults (which is usually the first thing we notice), we ask ourselves, "Who am I that anyone would want to follow me?" And so, we work hard to mask our faults, to bury them deep and cover them with a smooth veneer.

Unfortunately, when we do that, we become less authentic and less transparent and, therefore, less followable. It's a confounding paradox. The interesting thing, though, is that acknowledging your flaws doesn't mean you are complacent about them or aren't working to overcome them. In fact, acknowledging your flaws means that you recognize them, are owning them, and therefore (I propose) are further along than most in overcoming them.

Being willing to show your flaws allows your team to see you as human, honest, vulnerable and genuine. This almost invariably will garner respect and empathy, and your team will be more committed to working for you and with you.

When we work hard to seem perfect, others will work hard to find our flaws (if they give us any regard at all!). When we admit our shortcomings, others will naturally be drawn to us because we are more relatable, and they will work with us to help us grow.

"Being a strong leader doesn't mean you never ask for help. Only a bloated ego believes they never need help.

Ask for help so you can grow and be a better leader for your team."

When I was young, my parents purchased 3.5 acres on Vallecito Lake north of Durango, Colorado. We spent every summer for five years building a cabin in the back meadow of that plot of land. Having no degree or certification in construction, Dad somehow figured he could muscle through building an A-frame cabin that would be "good enough for government work." And it was *just* good enough. (It had so many things wrong with it!) We'd laugh and patch it up and laugh and patch it up again. It was wrong in so many ways, but it was ours, and we built it ourselves, so we loved it.

When I was in high school, The Colonel designed a house—his dream house. He wanted a home big enough that both of his daughters could bring their families for a visit at the same time and not feel crowded. Remembering the lesson from the cabin, Dad took his design to an architect and asked for help completing the plans and getting the permits. When it came time to build, Dad hired a construction foreman.

Every day, he and John would go over what Dad could do himself (so he could feel like he had built the house himself) and what was best left to "the professionals." Dad gathered a team of young men he knew needed income, guidance, or something to focus on—he always had several young men around that he was mentoring—and they built the house, with the help of "the professionals." When they experienced a challenge or got in over their heads, Dad would say, "Ya know what? Let's check with John before we go any further."

I know each member of Dad's hand-picked construction team would have been there to follow Dad and help him with whatever he asked them to do. And they respected him all the more for knowing what his limitations were.

"There are two types of decisions: good decisions and lessons learned."

The Colonel would never have been characterized as indecisive. In fact, he was a decision maker. Now, that doesn't mean he was rash in his decisions—quite the opposite. He always gathered all the evidence he could, did the research, weighed the options and then made what he believed would be the best decision. Sometimes his decisions were good, and sometimes they were not. But no matter what, he was always willing to make the decision and accept the consequences.

When I was struggling with the decision to quit my well-paying corporate job and start my own business or to stay put for a few more years, Dad encouraged me to just make a decision. I had weighed the pros and cons, the effect the initial loss of income would have on the family alongside giving up daycare and having more time at home for the kids and their school functions. I calculated how much it would cost to outfit an office with the essentials needed to run a business. I talked through all the ups and the downs I anticipated arising out of working from a solo home office, including the loss of office "socialization." Would I be motivated to actually work at home? Or would I be distracted by household stuff like neighborhood activities, laundry, cooking, and cleaning?

Finally, Dad put an end to the discussion: "Look, you're either going to do it or not. If you start your own business and you are a wild success, it was a good decision. If you discover that working out of your home office is not for you and you can't make it work, then it was a lesson learned, and you get a new job. This is not rocket science, kid." That about said it all. I quit my job and started my own business.

"We don't learn much when everything goes right. We learn most when things go wrong."

History is rife with stories of people who have "failed forward to success," as I would say. The Wright brothers failed initially, as did Albert Einstein, Thomas Edison, Alexander Graham Bell, Walt Disney, Abraham Lincoln, Michael Jordan, Franklin D. Roosevelt—the list could go on for the entire paragraph. The key to each of these ultimate success stories is that they all learned valuable lessons from their initial failures and put those lessons into practice to reach their eventual success.

During his lifetime, whenever I called The Colonel to admit to failure and talk it out, his initial question was always the same, "So, what have you learned, kid?" He never asked what I'd done wrong, but he always asked what I had learned. "Failure is only tragic," he said, "if you don't learn anything from it. If there is growth that comes from it, then we can live with it and move on."

Failure is a vital part of the growth process. Without it, any solution could be counted as a triumph, when there might have been a better, more successful alternative if you had simply failed a few times along the way.

Whether it is in sports, industry, science or art, the true giants in their field know that things go right more consistently if we learn from the times when things go wrong.

"What you do speaks so loudly I can't hear what you say.

Words are just words, kid. They don't mean anything if you don't stand by them with actions."

At one point in my career, I was very involved in a couple of Chamber of Commerce organizations in my area. As my travel time increased, I knew I needed to trim down my obligations to be more effective for my business. The decision of which to release, though, was difficult.

One particular chamber had just gone through a lengthy search process to find its new staff president. This new president talked about how valuable the membership was to her and how eager she was to get to know every one of us personally. I read everything she'd written, trying to find a glimpse into her character and authenticity, knowing that she would invariably set the standard for that chamber going forward.

At her first event, I introduced myself to her. We had a brief conversation, during the entirety of which she was looking over my shoulder at other people in the room. Though she met my eyes periodically on her way from looking over one shoulder to the other, it was never meaningful or focused. At breakfast, she said a few words from the podium and then introduced the speaker, who was a member of the chamber. After mispronouncing his name, she gushed apologies and said she couldn't wait to hear what he had to say.

The featured speaker was a banker, not a professional speaker, and it was apparent that he was very nervous. About two minutes into his presentation, the back of my brain was distracted by a conversation going on at the table behind me. Not a casual, "I missed that, what did he say?" kind of conversation, but a fully engaged, oblivious conversation. As a professional speaker, I certainly could hold my own in that situation, but this fellow was flustered.

I turned to see who was carrying on this rude conversation. (Okay, let's be honest, I turned to give them "the glare.") The oblivious conversation was coming from the new president.

My father's words came back to me, and the decision of which chamber to let go of was made.

"I don't have to agree with everything you say or do.

In fact, if we disagree now and then, we both have an opportunity to grow."

If everyone agreed all the time, the world would be a pretty boring place. Furthermore, it would be stagnant. There would be no reason to consider different perspectives or look at new ways to complete tasks.

Abraham Lincoln, who is heavily studied for his inherent and unconventional leadership skills, made a decision to fill his cabinet with rivals and dissenting voices. He expressed that, at a time when the country was in crisis, the last thing he needed by his side was a basket of "yes-men." This decision allowed him access to a very wide range of opinions which, he believed, would sharpen his own strategic thinking and analysis.

Creative problem solving is best achieved when people disagree. When we don't see eye to eye, we need to be willing to put everything on the table and take a good hard look at what our options are. Without differing opinions, the options are often limited to a few similar ideas.

Conflict is often what builds the character of the team and its individuals. Respectfully working through conflict provides an environment that can, with the right guidance, make the team stronger as a result. Making sure that everyone has a voice (even if it is the voice of dissent), and that everyone feels their voice is being respectfully heard, is a vital component of leadership.

Being open to dissenting opinions helps you build your strategic thinking, be open minded to different alternatives, and focus on what's best for the team as well as the organization.

"You need to believe in and be able to see possibility in your team before they can see it in themselves.

Trust me; if you believe in others before they have proven themselves, they will rise to the expectation."

The Colonel was a firm believer in stretching his daughters beyond what we believed were our limits, whether it was using the lawnmower when I was six or an ax to chop wood at twelve. He always challenged us to go further and do more than we believed we could. I won't say we always appreciated his extreme faith in us (and we may have called him a sadist more than once!), but we always managed to go beyond our own expectations.

One of the last movies The Colonel developed a passion for before he died was *Facing the Giants* (football, of course!). While the movie is formulaic and a bit sappy, it has a scene I will never forget. A failing high school football coach, Grant Taylor, is facing another losing season when he discovers the players' fathers and team boosters are plotting to have him fired. He has to find the right approach to turn the football team around when even they don't believe in themselves. The most memorable moment from this movie is when Coach Taylor challenges his star player to go 50 yards in a "death crawl" (only hands and feet, no knees) while blindfolded, with another player on his back. It is one of the most gut-wrenching scenes of sheer willpower I've ever seen. (*Spoiler alert!*) Because he is blindfolded, he can't see how far he's gone, and with his coach's encouragement, he keeps pushing and pushing until he crawls a full 100 yards and collapses into the opposite end zone.

I think Dad discovered that iconic "death crawl scene" before anyone else. He *loved* that grueling five and a half minutes of inspiration and watched it over and over again—as if each time he was unsure of the outcome.

He would revel in pride when the young Brock would go the distance because his coach believed in him more than he believed in himself.

If you never believe in someone before they show you what they are capable of, they will never stretch beyond what they think is possible. In fact, if someone has even the slightest fear of disappointing you, they will stay in their comfort zone so they know they can't fail.

Believe in others first, and then watch them rise to the expectation.

"One of the most important things you can provide to your team is safety—physical safety, emotional safety, intellectual safety.

They need to know you are their net."

As a kid, I was a climber. Trees, rock formations, towers I built out of sundry garage items—if it was going up, I would climb it. I never quite reasoned how I would get back down until I was already at the top. When we were stationed at Wright Patterson Air Force Base in Dayton, Ohio, there was a sprawling oak tree in a field across from our house. I was always in that tree, and Dad and I had a running bet as to how high I could climb. One day he came home from work to find me in the tree. I'd been sitting there for about an hour waiting for him to get home. I told him that I wanted him to see how high I had gone, but the reality was I had no idea how I was going to get back down!

Dad said, "I bet you could get to that next branch up there if you really tried."

"I don't know... what if I fall?"

"Then I'll catch you. Go ahead, give it a try. I've got ya."

Of course, I made it to that higher branch, and then The Colonel stood at the foot of the tree and spotted me for about 30 minutes as I navigated my way back to the ground. Afterward, we talked through the routes I tried that had failed initially, in comparison to the route that finally got me to the ground. I would never have reached that higher branch or felt willing to try to get down from my precarious perch had I not known he was there to catch me.

As a complement to believing in others first, it's important to let them know that they're in a space where it's safe to fail. Your team needs to know there won't be negative consequences if they try and fail; otherwise, they will never try.

Pushing past what you know you are capable of requires the assurance of a secure cushion to catch you when you fall short.

Your team needs to have the security of knowing you've created a safe environment in order for them to push beyond their own preconceived limitations.

"It's not weakness to admit when you are wrong, kid.

The strongest of leaders are willing to say, 'I was wrong' and 'I'm sorry.'"

It's not a prerequisite for leadership to always be right. If it were, there would be no leaders because *no one* is always right! Admitting when you are wrong takes so much more strength and so much more character than not doing so.

If you want your team to work effectively together—recognizing their own shortcomings, playing to each other's strengths, admitting when they are wrong and being willing to make amends to each other—they have to see that behavior modeled by their leader. You need to be willing to acknowledge your weaknesses, failures, and errors and be willing to apologize, taking action to make things right.

I have often done consulting work for people who believe that admitting they are wrong shows weakness or ineptitude. Unfortunately, this backs them into a corner where they are always defending their poor choices, even when they themselves have come to recognize that they were wrong. In order to save face, they have to place blame elsewhere in order to prove themselves right. This mindset is toxic to a team and erodes trust.

As a leader, it is incumbent upon you to model a willingness to admit mistakes, own up to shortcomings, acknowledge when you are wrong and make amends every time it's appropriate to do so.

"Your leadership will not be challenged when your team succeeds. That part is easy. It's when your team stumbles or fails—that's when you'll be tested as their leader."

Sir Ernest Shackleton is the best-known leader and explorer never to reach his destination. In 1901, Shackleton set out on a ship called the *Discovery* to explore Antarctica and reach the South Pole. He succumbed to frostbite and scurvy, however, and had to return home. Undaunted, in 1907 Shackleton set out again for the South Pole, this time on the *Nimrod*. Although they made it farther south than any person yet before them, this expedition fell 97 miles short of its target.

In 1912, Shackleton once again took charge of his destiny as captain of the *Endurance*—only to see her trapped by a shifting ice floe in the Weddell Sea for over eight months. The ice eventually crushed and sank the *Endurance*. Seemingly stranded there on the shifting ice, Shackleton rallied his crew, and they rowed lifeboats to secure landfall on Elephant Island. Still, there was little hope of rescue, because no one would know they were there. So, Shackleton took 5 of his crew and rowed 800 nautical miles to South Georgia Island, then hiked 32 miles across the island to reach a whaling station and arrange a rescue. A year and a half after first being trapped in the shifting ice floe, all 27 members of the crew were rescued, and every single one of them made it home alive.

When your crew (your team) is sailing in smooth, sunny waters, there is no real need for your leadership. It's when the seas grow rough and stormy, when the skies become dark and heavy, and when ice starts forming on your sails and bow that your team will look to you for focus, guidance, and salvation. It is your responsibility to be up to the challenge when it happens.

"Sometimes those who most need to be led are the ones who are least inclined to follow. Ya gotta find a way to make it matter to them."

While it is a normal and natural instinct to surround yourself with a team that thinks, believes, produces, and responds the way you do, it's not necessarily a great leadership characteristic. Great leaders know that differing perspectives, philosophies, and process-opinions create opportunities for growth and greater productivity. Differing opinions can provide fuel for a development and expansion of ideas not previously experienced.

Although it may seem easier to surround yourself with like-minded people, it is absolutely possible to effectively lead and build relationships with those who have different personality styles, communication characteristics, and generational experiences. This can happen with even the most adversarial of individuals.

Leading those who don't want to be led simply requires a more intense focus on understanding their needs, wants and desires. "Because I said so" will never achieve the desired result. Instead, put yourself in their shoes and try to figure out why the desired outcome would matter to *them*, and focus on that reasoning. Find common ground by listening and determining what makes them tick. Figure out what gets them revved up, and then find a way to incorporate that into the process.

While a leader's objective is to replace themselves, it should never be to clone themselves. Only by harnessing individual strengths can the whole team work together for the greater good of the organization. This is best accomplished by respecting and guiding individual talents, skills, inventiveness, and opinions, not by stifling them.

"Your team will look to you for more than just how to do their jobs. In many ways, they will look to you for how to live their lives. You have to be up to that measure as well."

No leader is perfect. That would be an impossible standard to aspire to. Leadership requires challenging yourself to be the best version of you every day—and then aspiring to be better tomorrow. Dad always said, "It takes a lifetime to build a reputation of character, and just one 'ah - #%$*' to tear it down."

In *Harry Potter and the Chamber of Secrets* by J. K. Rowling, the wise wizard Albus Dumbledore tells Harry, "It is our choices, Harry, that show what we truly are, far more than our abilities." Your team is watching your choices, your life choices as well as your work choices. They will not separate one from the other.

Leadership requires integrity, and integrity means doing what is right simply because it is right—every time, whether anyone is looking or not. But don't kid yourself, someone is always looking. Your team is observing you all the time to gain clues on how to work, how to treat others, how to communicate, how to handle tough situations, and how to hone their own character. If your behavior doesn't rise to their expectations—whether at work or outside of it—you will lose a fragment of your ability to lead. If enough fragments get lost, you will lose that ability altogether.

It's not your responsibility to be perfect, and it's not your job to parent your team. It *is* your responsibility, though to set the best example for them that you are capable of setting—because they're watching.

"If you can give them the *why,* the what and the how are gonna follow naturally."

As we move farther into the 21st century, the necessity for employees to be engaged becomes increasingly relevant. The 20th century concept of doing a task or a project just because your boss told you to is an antiquated and ineffective way to achieve productivity. Without a solid "why", you often end up with half-baked outcomes, shoddy performance, and minimal loyalty.

The Colonel understood this ahead of its time. He was a master at connecting the "if you do this, then this will happen" dots for his daughters and his staff. My sister and I were (are) very different people. As kids, Christi was intellectual and focused, while I was flighty and social. The reasons Christi did something (earning more allowance to put toward that car she'd been saving up for, perhaps) were very different from the reasons that I would do something (getting permission to join my friends at the park or the pool and stay there an hour longer than normal), and Dad would posture our incentives accordingly.

If you can communicate why your team wants to (or needs to) do something—give them the "what's in it for them"—then the means for achieving that task or project will usually come from them. It's imperative, therefore, that you get to know your team well, because one person's "why" may be very different from another person's. One size does not necessarily fit all.

A leader's job is vision building and vision casting. It's not always necessary for the leader to know the exact processes used to achieve that vision, especially if the team you've gathered is empowered to make their own decisions and find their own path to the outcome you have established.

"Always do the 'and then some,' and your team will do the same."

"Just enough" is never enough. If you want your team to go the extra mile, they have to see that you are willing to go the extra mile first. The Colonel modeled this truth to his daughters every day. We often called it "workaholism," and maybe there was a measure of that, but he was always the first to arrive, the last to leave, and the first to put in extra effort to get the job done.

Many of your well-meaning, high-ranking colleagues will tell you that if you're always putting in the extra effort, you are not taking advantage of the privilege of rank. They don't understand. Servant leadership is not about sitting back and letting your team do all the work. A leader doesn't have to do everything or be the best at everything, but a leader *does* have to be willing to do what needs to be done in order to achieve the goal for the team.

Sometimes, the "and then some" road is a lonely one, but it is the only road to excellence. In truth, some of your team may never join you on that road to excellence—and that's okay. The ones who step up to walk beside you are the ones who will themselves rise to leadership.

When your team sees you rolling up your sleeves and getting serious when they are on the verge of giving up, and when they see you doing more than you have to with an "attitude of gratitude," they will be empowered and inspired to do the same.

"Leaders are not born, kid. Leaders grow and evolve through practice, building skills and putting in the 'reps' until leadership is second nature."

While many believe there are people who are natural leaders, effective leadership is not a skill anyone is born with. It's something that requires study, time and effort to develop. As a child, I was always ready to take the lead, certain that I should be the one in charge (Maybe I was just bossy, who knows...), but that wasn't enough to make me a good leader. Leadership is a craft that requires skill. Skill requires practice. So, I had to put in the effort to learn the craft of leadership.

An example that Dad used often was professional golfer Tiger Woods. There's no question that the two-year-old Tiger, who appeared on the Mike Douglas show in 1978 and started slamming golf balls, was a child prodigy. However, that child prodigy would not have gained the reputation and accolades that Tiger Woods has without putting the "reps" in for all the skills involved in the game. At his prime, Tiger Woods employed up to four coaches at one time, each for different golf disciplines (driving, putting, wedges, etc.) and each of whom expected him to practice with them every day.

Any champion athlete learns from others and then works with coaches and mentors, putting in the "reps" and honing their craft until the skill becomes muscle memory.

It is the same with leadership. Stellar leadership requires working with mentors, consistently putting in the effort, and applying proven principles, over and over and over again.

Then, it begins to be muscle memory, and you don't have to think first before applying those proven principles. And, like any skill, leadership requires a willingness to be constantly learning and growing—to keep putting in the reps—so the skills don't become stagnant and atrophy.

"It's important to activate your brain *before* you drop anything into gear, kid."

This insight from The Colonel came, the first time, as he was teaching me to drive a manual transmission car. Later, he repeated it many times as I consulted him for insights on managing various teams throughout my corporate career.

Because of his size, and because he was continuously being called a "bull in a china shop," Dad was *very* keen on thinking things through before acting. He believed that there are two primary ways you could fail your team as a leader: The first was to think about doing something but never do it, and the second was to do something without thinking it through first.

Thinking of doing something, or worse, *talking* about doing something that you never actually put into action, will cause your team to question your resolve and your ability to implement. It's like shifting into neutral, dropping the clutch and revving the engine. There is a lot of noise and no motion. When you come across as tentative to your team, they eventually become less motivated, less empowered to proceed on their own, and, therefore, less productive. Once you have communicated an intent to act upon something, do it. Pick the gear and go with it.

On the other hand, plowing forward in action without thoroughly thinking things through to the end, and understanding how the action will affect all parties, is perhaps a greater mistake. Unfortunately, it's a mistake too many leaders make, believing it is important to be bold and purposeful. That is like shifting from first gear to fourth, bypassing second and third. That will kill the engine completely! You can be bold and purposeful without being rash.

As leaders, it's our responsibility to comprehensively consider everything that affects our team, to look at things from every angle, before moving forward in action.

"To lead effectively, you have to be humble enough to admit your mistakes, strong enough to fix them and smart enough to benefit from them."

You will make mistakes. *Everyone* makes mistakes. To pretend otherwise is just vanity, and when it does happen, it's important to acknowledge it.

Admitting a mistake is a hollow gesture, however, if you are not willing to buck up and fix the problem created by your mistake. If it has affected others, it's sometimes beneficial to solicit input from them about how to correct the error. It's possible that what you believe is an appropriate remedy is not what they want or need. This gives them a voice and guides them toward the healing process. It's imperative at that point for you to actually put into action the solutions they have recommended, or you must explain to them why you are going in a different direction and how that direction will affect them.

The last step is the most important in this whole process. Admitting mistakes and making them right is useless if we don't learn from them and find a way to create a positive from a negative. What is the silver lining and how can it be put to use to benefit your team, your organization, your community? Seeing you turn your lemon into a lemon meringue pie for the benefit of everyone will be a very valuable lesson to your team, while you are also learning and growing.

Be honest in admitting your mistakes and allow them to become teachable moments. This creates an atmosphere that is supportive of honesty and growth.

"You can have a brilliant vision, kiddo, but if you can't inspire others to action with that vision you're not a leader, just a dreamer."

For leaders to lead, it's not enough to have exceptional talent and vision, but you also need the ability to attract followers. By definition, you are not a leader if no one is following.

A couple of years ago, I saw a delightful video on YouTube. It took place at the Sasquatch Music Festival with many clusters of people picnicking and enjoying the afternoon. One lone, shirtless man is dancing an incredibly unusual rhythm to the music that is being piped over the loud-speaker. It is a comic and perhaps mock-able dance—until a second man gets up and joins him, trying to match him step for step. What happens next is amazing. The first dancer greets the second dancer, embracing him and showing him "his moves." This allows the two to dance together in simultaneous choreography rather than just as two people dancing side by side. That first follower transforms the lone, slightly crazy, dancer into a leader. If the leader is the flint, it is his first follower who creates the spark for the fire. Before you know it, a second follower joins them, and then momentum begins to build. Before long there are dozens of people all gyrating together in a spontaneous dance party. ("Sasquatch Music Festival 2009," by user Dkellerm—Look it up!)

How many "crackpot" ideas (landing on the moon, finding the Titanic, creating the world-wide-web) would never have been realized if the one with the vision could not effectively communicate what the vision looked like, inspiring others to action in following that vision?

Without followers, the first dancer is just "dreaming" in dance. He needed to be able to communicate his vision for what the dance looked like, how it flowed and what it meant before he could be called a leader of this dance movement.

"You aren't ever going to be perfect, kid. There is no such thing as a 'perfect leader.'

Just be a better leader today than you were yesterday, and better tomorrow than you were today."

I tend to lean toward perfectionism. While there are many benefits to having an obsessive attention to detail, perfectionism can be counterproductive in leadership for a couple of reasons.

First, expecting perfection from your team is setting a standard that they can never achieve, which is demoralizing. This eventually leads to poor morale, poor production, and attrition. Expecting excellence is a much better measure to use as a guide for your team's efforts.

The second challenge that comes with perfectionism is much subtler. Most perfectionists (myself included) understand at an intellectual level that no one is perfect. This allows us to give our team the slack they need to seek excellence instead. The insidious part comes from a gut or emotional level, which prevents us from giving ourselves that same slack. While not expecting perfection from our team, we somehow still expect it from ourselves. Your team sees this in you. They see you expecting more from yourself than you expect from them. If they respect and have affection for you, they will often push themselves to reach the standard you are setting for yourself, which can lead to mass burnout.

To avoid this trap, the message I tell myself is that I am "on target." You see, as a perfectionist, with every effort you put in, you improve and get better. A perfectionist never makes the same mistake twice. So, if you improve with every effort, then each improvement, small or large, means you are on target for the perfection you desire.

As long as you are on target for perfection, that gives you a framework wherein you can accept excellence for the time being and still feel good about yourself. Allow yourself to have that framework.

Strive for excellence from your team and accept excellence in yourself.

"I'm not gonna be in a leadership position forever, kiddo, and neither will you. No one is in leadership forever.

The best I, you, or anyone can hope for is to influence enough people that you create a legacy that outlives you."

When I assumed the board presidency of a non-profit, the organization was in a terrible state. I knew it was going to take a very complex balance of soft-glove and sledgehammer to get them back on a solid footing. The presidential term was one year, but in seeking The Colonel's counsel, I told him I thought I should ask the board for an extension up front and request a two- or three-year term. I thought it would take that long to stabilize the association. Dad advised me against it.

He said, "I know you, kiddo. You're gonna work your back-side off trying to turn it around in a year. Then you figure you'll have another year or two to create growth. And you'll kill yourself trying to make that happen. It's not your job to do it all yourself. It's your job to visualize the path that will take the association to where they want to be and help them take the first steps down that path."

He was right, of course. If I had done this, when we did stabilize the organization, it would have been seen as my success rather than the association's success. That's not leadership; it's solo achievement.

Instead, he encouraged me to work with the board to create a three-year plan that could be administered and guided by the next two presidents—creating footsteps for the subsequent presidents to walk in. This would have the double benefit of stabilizing and growing the organization, as well as growing the leadership skills of upcoming leaders.

"Ya gotta learn to be persuasive. Here's the difference between manipulation and persuasion. I manipulate you to benefit me. I persuade you to benefit *you* or the greater good of the team."

Early in my first supervisory position, I was deep into a "Lauren whining to her father" session. The subject was how my staff was not doing what I wanted them to do, or performing up to my expectations, or something to that general theme. Dad kept saying, "If they're not doing what you want them to do, you need to find a way to persuade them." Finally, in frustration, I said, "Dad, I am not a manipulative leader" (self-righteousness oozing out of every word...). That is when The Colonel explained the difference between persuasion and manipulation in the simplest, most profound manner: Manipulation is selfish. Persuasion is benevolent. I manipulate you to benefit me. I persuade you to benefit *you* or the greater good of the team.

I said, "Okay, but how do I persuade them without them thinking I am trying to manipulate them?" That's when he gave me the four keys to persuasion.

The first key is to build rapport. Every human being on earth has an invisible sign hanging around their neck that says, "Make me feel important." Read the sign. Let them know they matter as a person before anything else.

The second key is to ask, what's in it for them? How will it benefit them to improve their performance? How will it benefit them to make the change you want them to make?

How will it benefit them to buy into your idea or do things exactly the way you want them done? Frankly, they don't care how it's going to benefit you. Often, they don't care how it will benefit the company. How will it benefit them? Let them know what's in it for them.

The third key is communication. No one likes to be talked at, but everyone appreciates being communicated with. Make sure information is going both ways on the communication highway.

And, while communication is flowing both ways, the fourth key is to get their input. People will support what they helped to create, so get them involved with their input. You may not be able to act upon that input every time but be sure to always ask for it anyway.

These four keys allow you to be persuasive for the benefit of your employee, your team, and your organization.

"Communicating is not about speaking what we think. You'll know you've communicated yourself well when others hear what you mean."

It's no accident that I ended up as a professional speaker. It seems like I spent most of my youth hearing people tell me to stop talking. It wasn't until much later in my life that I realized there is a real difference between talking and communicating. Really communicating means that others hear the message behind the words; it compels others to internalize or act upon what you have said.

Like many people in high school, I read Robert A. Heinlein's book *Stranger in a Strange Land*. I was intrigued by many of the concepts put forth by the character Valentine Michael Smith, a human who is rescued after being stranded on Mars for twenty-five years, during which time he was raised by Martians. Having no previous exposure to Terran habits and culture, he brings with him seemingly eccentric ideas about religion, human eroticism, the afterlife, and communication.

As a teenager desperate to be understood, I was especially affected by the concept originally coined by Heinlein in the book: "grokking." To grok means to understand so fully, so intuitively, that empathy happens automatically. It is a complete grasping of all nuances of the message and what was intended in the communication. In the book, as in life, this is not something that happens quickly or easily. It must be cultivated and worked upon by two people on an on-going basis.

As leaders, we should always endeavor to communicate in such a manner that our team "groks." We should strive for an empathy bond such that, even when we word things poorly, our team can hear the message behind the words and hear what we truly mean.

"You may think I'm smart, and maybe I am. But all of my smarts and all my degrees don't amount to anything if I can't communicate in a manner that inspires and empowers others to act on what I've said."

Throughout my childhood, my father hammered into me the importance of being well spoken and having a broad vocabulary. During my grade school years, Dad gave me weekly assignments to look up words in the dictionary and then write out the definitions. This was a dual task, intended to both increase my vocabulary and improve my handwriting. In junior high, the weekly assignments grew, with the added goal of using the thesaurus to research and provide a minimum of five similar words that could be substituted without changing the overall meaning of a sentence. While I didn't appreciate it much as a kid, as an adult I am grateful for that forced expansion of my vocabulary.

Unfortunately, while I am proud of my advanced vocabulary, I am often chastised for "talking over peoples' heads." The interesting part of this critique (which I didn't realize until I became a speaker) is that it doesn't matter if you have an advanced vocabulary if you cannot successfully communicate your meaning. I have struggled against those who have advised me to "water down" my vocabulary to be more effective. I still struggle with it, even though I know they're right. As a speaker and one who aspires to be a master communicator, it does my audience no benefit if they lose my message because they don't understand every tenth word I say. Furthermore, it doesn't make me look smarter; it makes me come off as inauthentic.

It's our responsibility to express ourselves in such a manner that our message is easy to understand and causes the listener to internalize or act upon that message.

You can't inspire or empower someone with a message that goes over their head or that they don't understand enough to act upon. As leaders, it is our obligation to make sure we communicate our meaning successfully, so that we empower others to take action. Fancy words are only fancy if they can be fully grasped and used to inspire others to share your vision.

"Choose your team wisely. Pick people who have the knowledge, skill, and character to do what you need them to do. Once you've done that, step aside and let them do it."

We all have our strengths, and we all have our weaker areas. The mark of an outstanding leader is the ability to identify and surround themselves with people who are stronger in the areas where the leader is less developed. Doing so makes the whole team stronger.

Once you have gathered your dream team of skill and expertise, allow them to do what you hired them to do. Don't micromanage them. Nothing is more demeaning, degrading and demoralizing than being micromanaged, and doing so actually hinders productivity. The Colonel taught me that a micromanaging boss is just like a coach who still wants to be on the field—not effective as a player and less effective on the sidelines where he's supposed to be. When you get bogged down in analyzing and obsessing about procedures, one of two things will happen with your team. They will either be quietly rebellious, creating small, invisible ways to undermine you, or they will become hapless and unable to do anything without your detailed instructions and supervision. Either of these will prevent you from focusing on the important task of leading.

Instead, find the right people for the job; give it to them and let them do it. Take a step back and expand your view. Focus on effort and results rather than the minutia of specific processes. Even if they do things differently than you would have, as long as their process achieves the same result, let them do it any way that works for them.

Trust those you have delegated to. Shift from doing the work to leading conversations about the work. This allows you to expand your capacity while they build confidence and trust in you.

"Trust is built on telling the truth, not telling people what they want to hear."

Because I am inherently a people person (read: people pleaser), I have spent a good portion of my life and energy making sure people like me. Sometimes, in my younger years, this involved being agreeable and telling people what I knew they wanted to hear—even if it was not completely the truth, or even if it was a lie. It wasn't until the middle of my treatment for bulimia that I realized the truth is an uncompromising constant. It doesn't change based on what people want to hear. It just *is*. Every time you tell a lie, you have to remember what you told to whom. Eventually, that becomes unmanageable. Even "little bitty white lies" (like, "Oh, I'd love to, but I have plans") should not become a habit; they build a tenuous platform of glass that can easily crack if pushed on too aggressively. Don't say you'd love to if you wouldn't—and if you say you have plans, you'd better have plans. Because even if you make plans after the fact, when it came out of your mouth it was a lie, and that compromises the fabric of your integrity.

The challenging trick of leadership is finding a way to tell the truth in a manner that is easily digestible to the listener. Doing that is very different, however, than telling them what they want to hear. Sometimes the truth can be hard—but it should not be harsh. Finding a way to communicate hard truths without making the listener feel attacked, discounted or demeaned requires skill and practice.

Building a reputation as one who always tells the truth—even hard truths—without being harsh will build trust among your team.

"One of the most important sentiments any leader can express to someone in their charge is: 'I've got your back.'"

I love the moment in the classic movie *Spartacus* when Kirk Douglas (Spartacus) is about to give himself up to save the lives of the others. Before he can do so, Tony Curtis's character beats him to it, standing up and shouting, "I am Spartacus!" Then another man stands and also shouts, "I am Spartacus!" And then a third and fourth until the whole hillside of men are standing shouting that they are Spartacus. Spartacus was ready to be the first line of defense for his followers. Knowing that he would do that, they all stood—side by side—to protect him and each other.

As leaders, it is our responsibility to be the first line of defense for our team. That means we never throw our team members under the bus. When someone higher on the organizational chain wants blood, we stand in front of our team as a protective wall and take the heat ourselves. We don't question a team member's decisions in public. When we have given them the authority to make decisions, we support those decisions even if we don't agree with them. And unless they are illegal, immoral or unethical, we allow them to stand by their decisions without asking them to change them. If those decisions lead to bad results, we support them in picking up the pieces and learning from their mistakes.

This is how we build and mentor new leaders.

Having your team's back means you continually ask yourself, "Who do I need to be and what do I need to do to amplify my team's very best?" If you see them in distress, you offer to help, and you do so in a manner that ensures their difficulty will not be visible to anyone else.

As leaders, we are tasked with creating an environment where every member of our team knows categorically that the rest of the team has their back as well. Then, the entire team can work at their very best level.

"Cut through the emotion, eliminate the ego, cut out the clutter and the answer will usually be there."

The Colonel was very much a "cut to the chase" kind of thinker. He was very adept at slicing through irrelevant details to get at the core of the situation. (Because of this, I was rarely able to bamboozle him with a good story to avoid getting in trouble.) When I was in school, Dad would often help me with my homework. As I was struggling with fractions, Dad explained that understanding fractions was simply a matter of cutting out the clutter, by taking each fraction down to its simplest form.

He used the same process when tackling a seemingly complicated question or problematic situation. He taught me that solving and resolving anything is a simple matter of trimming the clutter.

Often, that clutter begins with emotions. If you are not in control of your emotions, you are incapable of looking at a situation objectively. Inflated egos will create clutter as well. Whatever the situation or the question, trim it down to its simplest form— just like finding the lowest common denominator in math.

It's like unraveling a knot one thread at a time. Some problems will take longer to unravel than others, but the process is valid regardless of the complexity. Unknotting a gnarled situation requires that we take the "I," the "you," and the emotion out of the situation. Trim the question down to its lowest common denominators—anything that is absolute fact in a situation—and the answer is usually there.

"Before anyone will give you a command, kid. You have to prove worthy of it. You have to be willing to follow before you can lead."

My first job out of college was as a receptionist for a major nationwide van line. I believe I was timid in my new role for about the first week. After that, I was certain that I knew it all.

During my annual review that first year, the General Manager's primary criticism of my work was that I was too eager to "drive the bus." He said, "Your job is to complete tasks on the bus as I ask you to. It's not to navigate; that's the Office Manager's job. It's not to do maintenance; that's the Operations Manager's job. *Driving* the bus is my job."

Naturally, I went home from that review and did what any good colonel's daughter would do—I called Daddy to whine. Dad promptly informed me that the General Manager was absolutely right. Then, Dad encouraged me to learn how to lead by first learning how to follow. I could be a leader among my co-workers by being the first to step up and work harder, by being supportive of my boss when no one else seemed to be, and by helping encourage my co-workers to run a little harder to hit our goals.

More than that, Dad explained, it was important for me to understand that I will always be answering to someone. My boss answered to the Regional Vice President. The

CEO of a company answers to the Board of Directors. The Chairman of the Joint Chiefs of Staff, the highest position in the United States Armed Forces, answers to the Commander in Chief. Even when I began my own business, I realized that although I work for myself, I answer to my clients and my audiences—or I don't get booked and hired again!

Before we can lead, we have to be willing to follow. Furthermore, we have to learn how to be a good follower, respecting authority and adhering to someone else's policies and procedures. We have to be willing to sit at the feet of great leaders and learn from them. We have to put in our time and do the practice it takes to earn responsibility.

"You can't just tell people where to go and expect them to go there. You have to be willing to go there yourself, and then make a compelling case for why they want to go there too."

The late Mary Kay Ash often said to her sales directors, "You cannot teach what you do not know, and you cannot lead where you will not go." It is probable that this quote is not original to Mary Kay, but she is the first person I ever heard it from. While I have often said that a leader doesn't need to know everything, or be the best at everything, it is ill-advised for any leader to expect their team to do something they are unwilling to do.

This concept was exhibited masterfully by the late Dr. Martin Luther King, Jr. He was more than willing to lead the march, be in the fray and do the work with the people he was leading. He was also consistently communicating a vision of what the world would look like when the goal was fully realized—how it would affect each African-American person—if those who could were willing to put in the effort to make it happen.

As leaders, we are responsible for establishing the vision and for guiding the team to that vision, and we are also tasked with communicating exactly how the achievement of that vision is going to affect and benefit each member of the team. What's in it for them? Sometimes, we also have to be willing to get into the trenches, to pull out a proverbial machete and hack through the undergrowth with our team, until they can proceed toward the vision on their own.

"Everyone has greatness in them, kid. You might have to dig deeper in some than in others to find it. You don't have to create greatness in your team. You just gotta find it."

I am an art history geek. My minor during my undergraduate work was in art history with a focus on the Renaissance and a specialty in the life and works of Michelangelo Buonarotti. One of Michelangelo's most famous works is the statue of David which he sculpted in 1504 on a commission from the City of Florence. There is an oft-told story about a time when Michelangelo was asked by Pope Leo X how he could have possibly imagined his magnificent *David* out of a massive, solid piece of Carrera marble. Michelangelo responded that the image was already in the marble; it had been placed in the stone by God. He said, "I simply remove everything that is not David."

While this exchange may or may not have actually taken place (it's not recorded in any historical reference work before the fiction piece *The Agony and The Ecstasy* by Irving Stone), it is an excellent illustration of this leadership principle.

To assume we are creating greatness in our team is ego-driven and steals the natural success from the team. If we take credit for their greatness, we must also be willing to take responsibility when that greatness does not emerge. Each member of your team has a unique set of gifts and skills embedded in them. Each of them has the possibility of greatness. It is not a leader's job to create the possibility, merely to nurture it. For some team members, that probability is bubbling very close to the surface. For others, it is more possibility than probability and more "marble" needs to be removed for the greatness to emerge. Sometimes, it is our job to chip away at the marble in preparation for another leader, sometime down the road, who will continue inspiring and empowering them, thus helping finish the masterpiece.

Our job as leaders is to mentor our team to find the greatness that is already inside of them.

"Everyone dreams of making a name for themselves, Kiddo, and I know you will. But you don't have to be a world-wide name to be a good leader. Start where you are. Leadership is a series of small, daily choices that people make [illegible] you to be [illegible]."

"Everyone dreams of making a name for themselves, kiddo, and I know you will. But you don't have to be a worldwide name to be a great leader. Start where you are. Leadership is a series of small, daily choices that inspire those around you to be their best."

I think at one time or another every child dreams of being famous. I certainly did. (I wanted to be a theater and film star.) Few actually achieve global name recognition, and many who do are not leaders in any way. The good news is being a great leader doesn't require fame or notoriety.

Miep Gies was a foster child who later became a secretary in a spice plant in Amsterdam. She was a relatively invisible member of society who made a life-changing decision. Faced with the potential of what she believed to be a horrible wrong, she decided to protect a family that would have otherwise been arrested and executed by the Nazis. She made a series of small daily choices that included where to buy food for the hidden family, how much she could buy each day without suspicion, when to make deliveries to them, and how to dispose of their waste. Any error in judgment could have cost her life. For two years, she, her husband and a handful of trusted others protected the Franks until they were betrayed by someone at the spice plant and discovered.

After the Franks were arrested, Gies retrieved Anne's diary and kept it safe until after the war when she returned it to Anne's father, Otto, the only surviving family member. The name Anne Frank, the 13-year-old who went into hiding, is known worldwide. Few people know the name of the woman who facilitated their concealment for two years, but that doesn't make Miep Gies any less of a leader for having selflessly orchestrated their protection.

Harriett Tubman was a woman of small stature and, by all accounts, homely appearance. She was illiterate and poorly spoken. She was permanently maimed and walked with a limp due to consistent beatings at the hand of her master. And yet, her commitment to the cause of freedom and her leadership skills brought roughly 70 people out of bondage through the Underground Railroad toward the end of the Civil War. The descendants of those she led to freedom count in the multiple tens of thousands. Today, Tubman is well remembered and admired for her courage and her leadership. At the time, she simply worked tirelessly and quietly to lead people to freedom by giving them a vision of what their lives could be if they made the dangerous journey north.

The Colonel was a tremendous leader, and yet few outside of the USAF and our circle of friends and family knew he existed. You don't have to be famous to be a leader. You just need to lead.

"A manager will give you something to work on. A leader will give you something to work toward."

Dad was very adamant about the difference between being a manager and being a leader. He was correct in that assessment. I have met and worked with many managers who are not leaders in any way. A manager can tell someone what to do, when to do it, and even how to do it. It takes a leader to inspire them to want to do it. Managers focus on production and numbers. Leaders focus on development, growth, and relationships.

A team can be committed to the organization, getting along well, and doing great work, but if they aren't moving toward a shared vision, they are not as effective as they could be. Like players on a football team, every member of your team has a specific job to do. On a football team, some may be rushing, some may be blocking, some may be tackling, etc., but they all have a common vision, a common objective—and that is to get the ball into the end zone and score (or prevent the other team from doing so). Without that common objective to work toward, the individual skills would result in nothing more than just a bunch of men being physically aggressive with each other on a grassy field.

One of the primary jobs of leadership is providing a vision for where the team is going and what it's going to look like when they get there. Each member of your team needs to know both the individual parts they play (the "what are you working on?") and how they will share the benefit at the end (the "what are we all working toward?"). Tell them how it's going to feel when we achieve "X" together. When you focus on that common goal, the team will grab that vision and start running toward it.

"Sometimes leadership means saying no when it would be so much easier to say yes."

As my two children grew into adulthood, I can't count how many times I have said no to something, battled the emotion, the arguments, the hysterics, the cold shoulder, and then stood my ground when it would have been so much easier to just give in to whatever was being asked of me. When I knew it was in the best interests of my child to say no, and I knew that holding to that best interest line would make me the "worst mom in the whole world," I still had to make the best choice, not necessarily the easiest.

While leadership is *not* parenting, there are many correlations. When I look back at how The Colonel parented me, it's easy to see the leadership principles he utilized—and therefore instilled in me. (Hindsight is a marvelous thing, isn't it?)

One of my recent clients had an employee who was very good at her job but still had some growing and maturing to do. This employee believed that, because of her hard work and her skill, it was time for her to move into a lead or, better yet, a supervisory position. My client knew she would fail miserably in a supervisory position because she lacked the emotional maturity to lead a team effectively. The employee argued and cried and threatened to take this "discrimination" to Human Resources. It was a very difficult situation for my client, but he knew that it was his responsibility to look out for the best interests of both this employee and any team she might lead. Regardless of how difficult it was, the answer was no. Instead, we worked together to devise and implement a growth plan for her emotional intelligence and basic leadership skills.

Often saying no is *way* more challenging than saying yes. As leaders, it's our responsibility to know what's best for individual team members and the whole team, then buck up, ride through the rough road, and say no.

"People will be watching you. They will measure your character by the way you treat those who report to you."

"People will be watching you. They will measure your character by the way you treat those who report to you."

Dad believed the measure of a human being is, in large part, how they treat the people who can't do anything for them. It's easy to treat people well if we want or need something from them or if they are perceived to be in a higher position than we are. It's how we treat the rest of the population—those who report to us or who are lower in the organizational chart—that really defines us.

When I first joined the National Speakers Association, I was relatively green and eager to learn the ins and outs of the speaking business. NSA was founded on the premise that, as we help each other get better, the whole speaking industry gets better and grows as a result. During my first six months in the association, I met many people who had achieved what I was hoping to achieve. Some dismissed me entirely as not worth their time, while others saw me as a rookie target and were eager to sell me their consulting services on how I could become a million-dollar speaker. Those who really took a genuine interest in me, with an authentic desire to help me build my potential, were few and far between. One speaker in particular had been in the business for over 25 years. He offered his time, expertise, insights, contacts and marketing resources to help me build to a level where (theoretically) I didn't need him anymore. He has never expected anything in return. Of course, we have become very good friends, and I will always need him in that capacity. I respect and admire him a great deal.

Now that I have achieved a portion of the success I aspire to, I am often approached by emerging speakers wanting to "pick my brain" and ask questions. While my time is valuable, I always take the time to offer whatever wisdom I can. I gauge how I treat the up-and-comers based upon how I was treated and endeavor to make them feel valued while giving freely to help them build their own success.

Furthermore, I find many of those who dismissed me initially wanting to get to know me and build collaborations or partnerships. Because I now have a solid indication of how they will treat smaller-fish clients and session participants who, perhaps, have no further connections for them, I pick and choose who I respond to very carefully.

How you treat those who report to you and those who seemingly can do nothing for you is a measure of your character, and people notice.

"Sometimes you have to give up the spotlight, kiddo.

Ya know, the orchestra conductor has to turn his back on the audience to effectively lead the musicians."

This was a hard leadership lesson for me to internalize. For as long as I can remember, I have been a "front and center stage, spotlight please..." kind of person.

It is not always an effective leadership quality.

In the theater, the director selects the cast, those actors he believes will be perfect in the roles he has selected. He provides the vision for the overall look of a production. He determines the actors' movements and guides how the emotions of each scene should flow. The director watches as the cast builds on his vision and offers notes at the end of each rehearsal on how the show can be improved. Once that's done, the director steps back and allows the cast to shine. You don't see the director on stage during the performance, and you rarely, if ever, see the director take a curtain call.

While we may think a leader should always be out in front leading the way, more often than not it's the leader's job to step aside and allow the team to shine, while offering support and guidance from the wings.

"Don't tell your team what kind of leader you are. They won't follow you because of what you say. Show them what kind of leader you are in your attitude and your behaviors. They *will* watch and follow you because of what you do."

I believe there are three ways to lead: by example, by example, and (you guessed it) by example. When a leader talks about how the team should treat each other with respect, and then disrespects someone, all credibility is lost. The team gets the message very clearly that it's actually okay to disrespect each other, regardless of what was said. If the leader rallies the team together for a "we've all got to work harder" speech, and then takes the afternoon off, the message that's actually sent is very different than what was intended.

On the other hand, when the team sees their leader treating each person with respect, they will be more likely to follow that example. When the leader says, "We've all got to work a bit harder to make this happen," and then rolls his shirt sleeves up, digs in and actually works harder himself to get things done, the team will be motivated to work harder as well.

In leadership, there is no space for, "Do as I say, not as I do." Your team is always watching and will follow your example, whether you want them to or not.

"Stop talking. Listen. You don't learn anything from talking. But if you listen, one way or another your team will tell you what you need to know about them and what they need."

I have been a talker my whole life. Dad often said, "Lauren Ann, stop talking just to hear the sound of your own voice." Those of us with the "gift of gab" are, for some irrational reason, afraid of silence—and so we tend to fill it with words ourselves. This is an area where I have really had to work on disciplining myself. I still have to work at it.

St. Francis of Assisi, and later Dr. Stephen Covey, advised that we should "seek first to understand." It's very difficult to do this if your mouth is working harder than your ears. If you are always the one talking, your team eventually stops listening. It becomes a monologue rather than a dialogue—and often a monologue to a brick wall.

Try to stop talking and listen for a while instead. Furthermore, when you listen, turn off your internal dialogue—you know, the one that's always interrupting with, "Yes, but..." Listen with the intention of listening, not with the intention of responding. This, more often than not, allows you to hear the message behind the words.

When you do this, your team will begin to share more about their projects, their struggles, their joys, their frustrations, and their aspirations. They will begin, in subtle ways, to express how they need to be led, when and how they need encouragement, and when they need to be left alone to figure it out on their own.

They will tell you what they need from you—but only if you are listening more than you are talking.

"You have to keep educating yourself. If you're not always learning and growing as a person, you're not growing as a leader."

The Colonel had two master's degrees and a Ph.D. He was a committed, life-long learner, and he instilled that expectation in his daughters. I believe once we stop learning we start dying, so I am continually looking for more information in my areas of expertise. I study new systems and methodologies, and I study how to improve my stage-craft and how to refine my business practices. The more I continue to learn about what I present, and how it affects a continuously evolving workplace, and the more I refine how I present that information, the more effective I can be for my consulting clients and the people who hire me to speak.

As leaders we have to keep learning and growing, both as people and as leaders. We need to be improving continually—in our communication skills, our strategic thinking, our insights into our competitors, and our understanding of industry trends, technology, and human resource trends (if not actually HR law).

I heard a joke when I was a sales director with Mary Kay Cosmetics that went something like, "There goes my team. I must follow them, for I am their leader!" While that may cause a chuckle, I wonder how many leaders feel that way because they have stopped educating themselves daily.

You don't have to know absolutely everything about everything—that is an unattainable expectation. To retain the right to lead, however, we do have to be committed to continual growth and continual learning.

"You've got to be an optimist. When your team can't see the light at the end of the tunnel, you have to be able to show it to them and convince them it's not a train."

Optimism is not a squishy, overly idealist characteristic. Optimism is actually a hard-core discipline. An optimist sees negative situations as temporary and surmountable, while seeing positive situations as permanent and sustainable.

I love what Henry David Thoreau said in his book *Walden*: "If one advances confidently in the direction of his dreams, and endeavors to live the life which he has imagined, he will meet with a success unexpected in common hours." That should be the vision statement of an optimist!

No vision or plan happens without obstacles and setbacks. Optimism allows a leader to stay committed to that vision when facing adversity. It requires believing in your team and knowing they can rise above the obstacle and still succeed. An optimistic leader can help boost employee morale, enhance productivity and overcome setbacks just by believing in a successful outcome.

When you believe there is *always* a route to success, it eliminates the fear of failure and challenges your team to find that route, even if it may end up looking different than originally expected.

"Leadership is not supposed to be comfortable, kid. It's supposed to challenge you, frustrate you, keep you on your toes and force you to grow."

Throughout my career, I have always pushed myself to obtain a leadership position. There have been a few times, though, when I have wondered why I do it. The first time I was ready to throw in the towel altogether, I called Dad. He was not nearly as sympathetic as I hoped he would be. He didn't offer me condolences for my wounded feelings or coddle me in any manner. He did, on the other hand, offer me empathy. Leadership is hard, he agreed—and nobody ever said it would be easy.

He encouraged me to look at the other side of the coin. If no one was willing to be uncomfortable in leadership, there would be no rudder for the ship to point the direction, guide the path, and keep everyone enthusiastic about the destination. The German philosopher Friedrich Nietzsche said, "That which doesn't kill us makes us stronger." Although I really hated it every time The Colonel repeated that quote, there is merit in it. Allowing yourself to be frustrated and challenged—sticking through it and coming out on the other side—hones your leadership skills so that next time, the same situation will not be quite so challenging or quite so frustrating.

Leadership is not easy. It's not comfortable. It *is* incredibly rewarding.

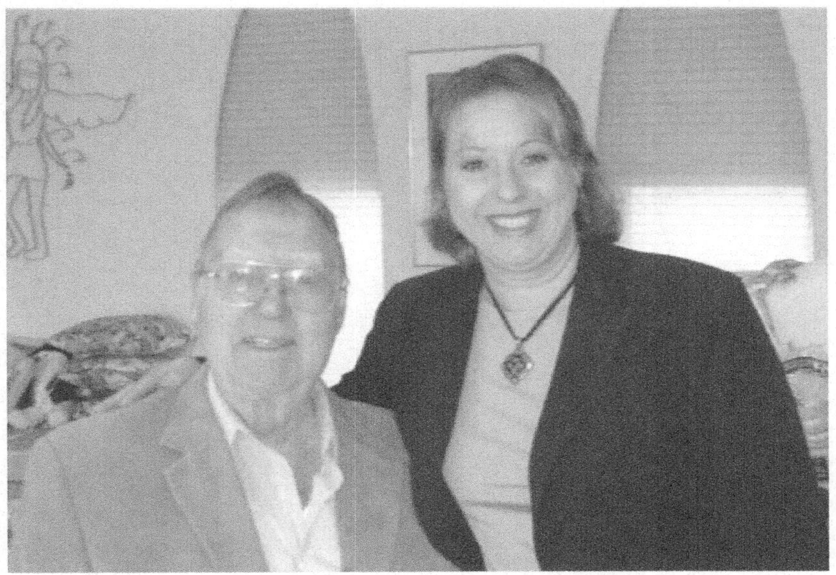

This is the last picture Dad and I took together, just before he passed.

Acknowledgments

All praise, honor and glory go to my Father in Heaven who is bigger, stronger, wiser, and more patient even than The Colonel and who crafted me for a specific purpose.

Thank you, **Jenny Ashton**, for consulting with me when I was in the midst of a brand crisis and showing me what was in front of my face: that who I am and what I espouse all came from one guiding mentor. I *am* The Colonel's Daughter.

Thank you, **Lindy Rosenson**, for believing in and visualizing the future business that we could build together. You are an outstanding Booking Manager and an even better friend.

Thank you, **Ron Schieffer**, for always being willing to proofread my work before I send it to an editor. And for doing it (for the most part) on my time schedule. I know you would rather just sit and let your brain relax. I appreciate and love you more than I can ever express.

Thank you, **Nibal Henderson**, for being there when I was experiencing a crushing lack of faith in myself. When I was on the verge of throwing in the towel, you looked me in the eye and told me to "cut that crap out." I love you for that.

Thank you, **Steven Iwersen**, for making the casual request for a copy of my "Colonelisms," which got this entire ball of memories rolling into a book.

Thank you, **Ed Robinson**, for your support, your counsel, your mentoring and your perpetual willingness to share what you know and have learned in order to help make my business better.

Thank you to the Board of Directors of the Kansas City Chapter of the National Speakers Association: **Marquita Miller, Dr. Troy Nash, Mary Redmond, Candy Whirley, Cary Phillips** and **Steven Iwersen**, for being a family of friends and professionals I know I can *always* count on.

ABOUT THE AUTHOR

As the daughter of a career Air Force officer, Lauren Schieffer, CSP, gained a profound independence and ability to adapt to changing circumstances with grace and humor. She shares lessons learned from "The Colonel" and 20 years in business with corporations, associations, and not-for-profits across the globe.

Able to relate to and energize everyone from custodial staff to the C-suite, Lauren is a master storyteller, delivering insightful and relevant content that empowers people to absorb and act upon what they've heard—and she does so with a dry sense of humor that keeps them chuckling while they're learning.

Her enthusiasm is infectious and her passion unmistakable.

Made in the USA
Middletown, DE
04 June 2020